Taking Your Camera to FRANCE

Ted Park

D1301280

Steadwell Books

Raintree Steck-Vaughn Publishers

A Harcourt Company

Austin · New York
www.steck-vaughn.com

Published by Raintree Steck-Vaughn Publishers,
an imprint of Steck-Vaughn Company

Library of Congress Cataloging-in-Publication Data
Park, Ted
        Taking Your Camera to France / Ted Park
            p.   cm. — (Taking Your Camera to)
        Includes index.
        Summary:
ISBN 0-7398-1800-7

Printed in the United States of America
10 9 8 7 6 5 4 3 2   02 01 00

Cover photo: A view of Paris taken from Nôtre Dame Cathedral

Photo acknowledgments
p.i (c)Jean Kugler/FPG International; p.3 (Eiffel Tower) (c)CORBIS; p.3 (boy) (c)Arthur Tilley/FPG International; p.3 (girl) (c)Corel; p.4 (c)Chris Salvo/FPG International; p.7 (both) (c)Cartesia Software; pp.8, 9 (c)Telegraph Colour Library/FPG International; p.10 (c)CORBIS; p.11 (c)Telegraph Colour Library/FPG International; p.13 (c)Tom Craig/FPG International; p.15 (both) (c)Corel; p.17 (castle) (c)Jean Kugler/FPG International; p.17 (train) (c)Telegraph Colour Library/FPG International; p.19 (c)Vladimir Pcholkin/FPG International; p.23 (c)AP/Wide World Photos; p.25 (c)Arthur Tilley/FPG International; p.27 (c)Stephen Simpson/FPG International; p.28 (Paris) (c)Telegraph Colour Library/FPG International; p.29 (beach) (c)Telegraph Colour Library/FPG International; p.29 (map) (c)Cartesia Software. Additional photos (c)PhotoDisc.

All statistics in the Quick Facts section come from *The New York Times Almanac* (1999) and *The World Almanac* (1999)

Contents

This is France

France is a large country in Europe. It has tall mountains. It has grassy plains. It has sandy beaches. If you took your camera to France, you could take photographs of many things.

France has many interesting cities. One of them is Paris, the capital of France. Paris has many famous sights you can photograph. One of these is the Eiffel Tower. Another is the Arc de Triomphe.

The Arc de Triomphe is a well-known sight in Paris.

In the countryside, you might see grapevines being trimmed.

France also has beautiful countryside. There you could see some of France's farms. You might see land where grapes are grown. You might even see places where cheese is made.

This book will show you some of these places. It will also tell you much about the country of France. When you take your camera to France, you will enjoy your visit more.

5 📷

The Place

France is the second-largest country in Europe. It is about 500 miles (805 km) from north to south and the same from east to west. This is about the size of the states of Colorado and Wyoming together.

Much of France borders the sea. To the north is the English Channel. The Atlantic Ocean is to the west. On the south is the Mediterranean Sea. Fishing is important in all these places.

Along part of the southern coast of France is an area called the Riviera. There are many sandy beaches and vacation places here.

France has different kinds of land. Much of France is made up of grassy plains. This is where a lot of the farming takes place. Forests cover about one fourth of the country. France has many rivers. Canals join many of them. The canals make it easy for boats to sail from one part of the country to another.

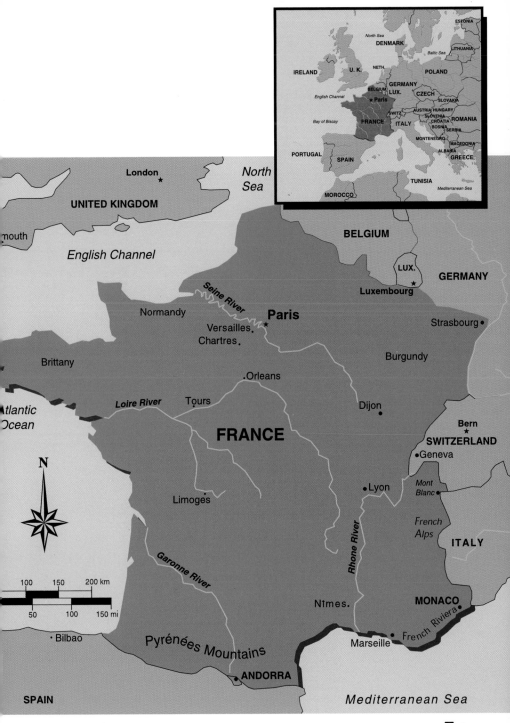

ESTONIA
North Sea
DENMARK
Baltic Sea
LITHUANIA
IRELAND   U. K.   NETH.   POLAND
BELGIUM   GERMANY
LUX.   CZECH
English Channel   ★ Paris   SLOVAKIA
AUSTRIA HUNGARY
SWITZ.   SLOVENIA   ROMANIA
Bay of Biscay   FRANCE   CROATIA
ITALY   BOSNIA   SERBIA
MONTENEGRO   MACEDONIA
PORTUGAL   ALBANIA
SPAIN   GREECE
TUNISIA
MOROCCO   Mediterranean Sea

London ★   North Sea
UNITED KINGDOM
mouth
English Channel   BELGIUM
LUX.   GERMANY
Luxembourg ★
Seine River
Normandy   Paris ★   Strasbourg •
Versailles •
Chartres •   Burgundy
Brittany
• Orleans
Loire River   Tours •   Dijon •
Atlantic   FRANCE
Ocean
Bern ★
SWITZERLAND
N   • Geneva
Limoges •   Lyon •   Mont Blanc •
French Alps
ITALY
Garonne River   Rhone River   MONACO
100   150   200 km   Nîmes •   French Riviera
50   100   150 mi   Marseille
• Bilbao   Pyrénées Mountains
ANDORRA
SPAIN   Mediterranean Sea

France has many mountains. The Pyrénées Mountains in the south divide France and Spain. In the east are the French Alps. The Alps have some of Europe's tallest peaks. The highest of these is Mont Blanc. It is 15,771 feet (4,807 m) high.

The high peaks in the French Alps are a beautiful sight.

 8

Much of France has a temperate climate. This means that in most places it is fairly mild much of the year. However, in the mountains there can be a lot of snow. Along the Mediterranean, it is hot almost all the time.

The French Riviera is a popular vacation spot. You could take a picture of one of its sandy beaches.

9 📷

Paris

The capital of France is one of the best-known cities in the world. Many people come here from all over the world. Paris is full of wide streets, green parks, and old buildings.

One of the most famous sights is the Eiffel Tower. It was opened in 1889. Many visitors take the elevator to the top.

The Eiffel Tower is among the most popular places in Paris. It is 984 feet (300 m) tall.

The Arche de la Défense

Paris has many museums. The most famous is the Louvre. People go here every day to see its many works of art.

If you take your camera on the streets of Paris, you can photograph all sorts of sights. One of them is the Arc de Triomphe. It is at one end of a wide street. The street is called the Champs-Elysées. The arch was built in 1836. Farther along is another arch. It is known as the Arche de la Défense. This arch was opened in 1989. These two arches show the old and new in Paris.

 Places to Visit

In ancient times, France was a colony of the Roman Empire. It was known as Gaul. The Romans built many things while they were in France. One of the most famous is an aqueduct in Nîmes, a city in southern France. An aqueduct carries water to places where it is needed.

A favorite place to visit in Paris is Nôtre Dame. This famous cathedral took almost 200 years to build. More than 6,000 people can go to a service here. Visitors can climb to the top of Nôtre Dame to take photographs of the city of Paris.

Louis XIV (14th) was a king of France. He ruled from 1643 to 1715. During his time as king, he lived in the palace at Versailles. The palace is about 15 miles (24 km) from Paris. It has many beautiful large rooms.

The gardens of Versailles are known for their fountains.

The People

There are almost 60 million people living in France. They are a mix of many peoples. Invaders from the far north came to the region of Normandy in northern France. Brittany is in the northwest corner of the country. The people who live there are called Bretons. These people speak a language that is like Welsh or Irish. The people who live in the Pyrénées are known as Basques. They also speak a language that is not French.

France has many immigrants. They move from other countries to make their homes in France. Some of these immigrants are from places that France once ruled. These include such places as Vietnam, Algeria, Tunisia, and Morocco. The immigrants bring their food and customs with them. These different people make France a very interesting country.

A man in **Paris** is carrying his bread and cheese.

This young girl is from **Burgundy**, a region in the east of France.

15 📷

# Life in France

Many French people live in cities. Many of them live in small apartments. Some people live in the countryside.

To the French, family life is important. French workers get about six weeks of vacation each year. They like to spend their vacations with their families.

Some families may visit other countries. Other families like to travel in France on their vacations. They can do this easily because France has good, fast trains. The trains are known as TGV, which stands for Train à Grande Vitesse. In English, this means "fast train."

When the French travel in their own country, they can see signs of the past. Many cathedrals are in the centers of small towns. Old castles are known as châteaus. They are found throughout the land.

The French countryside has many old châteaus. They make good photographs.

One of France's fast trains, known as TGV, races through France. It will take you to many places quickly.

17

 Government and Religion

France has been a republic since 1789. This means that the leader, or president, is elected. Elections take place every seven years. Then the president appoints a prime minister. This person helps the president run the country. There are two groups that make laws. They are the National Assembly and the Senate. The citizens of France elect these people.

Most French people are Roman Catholics. France also has about four million Muslims. Many of these Muslims used to live in France's African colonies.

You can photograph many cathedrals in France. This is the cathedral and old town of Chartres.

 18

# Earning a Living

In France people have many different types of jobs. Farming is an important industry. This is because there is so much good farmland in the country. France is Europe's largest grower of wheat, barley, and corn. Farms used to be small, and the work was done by hand. Now machines do most of the work.

Wine is another important industry in France. France makes more wine than any other country. It is France's biggest export. This means that France ships more wine overseas than any other product. Most of the grapes used to make wine are grown in the east and the south.

Still another important industry is space technology. Others include the car, chemical, and electrical industries. The airplane industry is also important. The Airbus is fast becoming one of the world's popular airplanes. It is built in France.

The French make fine perfumes and clothing. You can buy these products all over the world.

Another industry is the service industry. This provides many jobs in hotels, restaurants, and transportation. Some 52 million visitors come to France each year. It is important that they are treated well.

If you visit the grape-growing countryside, you can photograph workers such as these.

School and Sports

Young people in France have to go to school from ages 6 to 16. Then they may go on for two more years, until they are 18. During these two years, students go to schools called lycées. They are like high schools. Most children go to school for a full day. At age 18, students may go on to college.

Many French people enjoy sports. Bicycling is a very popular sport in France. Each year a bike race takes place. It is called the Tour de France. The race goes all over the country and takes about three weeks. Car racing is another favorite French sport. The yearly Le Mans race gets much attention. This race takes 24 hours. Soccer is the favorite team sport. French people also enjoy skiing, boating, and horseback riding.

Races are exciting events to photograph. This is a photo of the Tour de France at the Arc de Triomphe in Paris.

Food and Holidays

The favorite bread in France is a baguette, made in a long loaf. Croissants are rich rolls made of eggs, flour, and butter. They are enjoyed in other parts of the world as well. Quiche is a French dish that has become well known in many places. Quiche is a mix of eggs, cream, and cheese that is baked in a pie shell.

The most important holiday to the French is Bastille Day. It is on July 14. This date marked the beginning of the French Revolution. Peasants rose up against the people who ran the country. The peasants attacked the Bastille, a prison in the center of Paris. They let the prisoners go. Today, on Bastille Day, there may be parties, parades, and fireworks. If you visit France on Bastille Day, you can take photographs of the many things that happen on this holiday.

Most French people celebrate Easter and Christmas. These are religious holidays. Other holidays are sometimes celebrated in certain places. These holidays often honor what farmers grow in their region. Sometimes fruits, wines, or cheeses are the center of these holidays.

A young child carries home some baguettes.

# The Future

If you took your camera to France, you would see a country that is changing. Many new things are happening there. Travel times from Paris to London are getting shorter. The Channel Tunnel helps people go from Paris to London. It now takes just three hours to go between these cities.

France has long been a world leader in the peaceful use of nuclear power. Cheap electricity comes from the many nuclear plants in France.

However, like other nations, France has some problems. In many industries, people are slowly being replaced by robots. There are many cars on the roads of France. They can pollute the air.

The people of France want to solve these problems. They are proud of their country. They look to the future with excitement. As the French say, "Vive la France." In English this means, "Long live France."

The new glass pyramid is in front of the Louvre in Paris.
This is an example of the old and the new side by side.

Quick Facts About
FRANCE

Capital
Paris

Borders
Belgium, Luxembourg,
Germany, Switzerland, Italy,
Spain. Andorra and Monaco
are also part of France.

Area
210,026 square miles
(543,925 sq km)

Population
58.8 million

Largest cities
Paris (2,152,423 people);
Marseille (800,000 people);
Lyon (415,847 people)

Chief crops
cereal grains, sugar beets,
potatoes, wine grapes

Natural resources
coal, iron ore, bauxite

Longest river
Loire, at 634 miles (1,020 km)

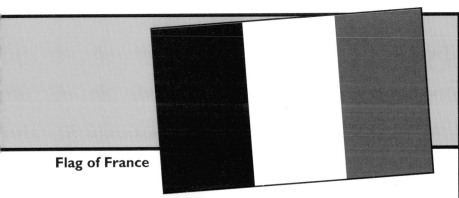

Flag of France

◀ **Coastline**
2,130 miles (3,428 km)

Monetary unit
French franc

Literacy rate
83 percent of the French can read and write.

Major industries
steel, machinery, chemicals, cars

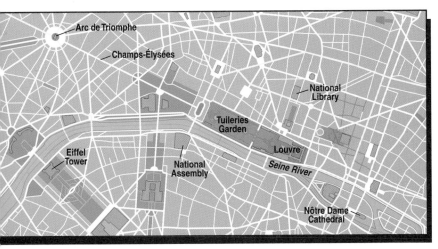

Arc de Triomphe
Champs-Élysées
National Library
Tuileries Garden
Louvre
Eiffel Tower
National Assembly
Seine River
Nôtre Dame Cathedral

Map of Paris

Glossary

Arc de Triomphe (ark duh TREE-ompf) An arch in the center of Paris built many years ago

Arche de la Défense (arch du lah DAY-fawns) A new arch in the center of Paris

baguette (bah-GETTE) A loaf of French bread

Bastille (bas-STEEL) An old prison in Paris

Bretons (BREH-tawns) People who live in Brittany

Brittany (BRIT-uh-nee) A region in northern France

Champs-Elysées (SHAWNS el ee-ZAY) A wide main street in Paris

Chartres (shart) A town southwest of Paris with a famous cathedral

colony Land that has been settled by people from another country

croissants (KWA-sahns) Rolls made of flour, eggs, and butter

Eiffel Tower (EYE-fuhl) A famous steel tower in Paris

export Goods that are sent out of a country

immigrant A person who comes to a country from another country to live

 30

industry The making of goods

Le Mans (luh manz) A famous automobile race

Louvre (loove) An art museum in the center of Paris

lycée (lee-SAY) A school, much like a high school

Nîmes (neem) A town in southern France

Normandy (NOR-mun-dee) A region in northern France

Nôtre Dame (NO-truh dam) A famous cathedral in Paris

Pyrénées (peer-ih-NAY) Mountains that separate France from Spain

quiche (keysh) A pie made from cream, eggs, and cheese

republic A government whose leader is elected

Riviera (riv-ee-AIR-uh) An area on the south coast of France

Tour de France (toor duh frawnse) A well-known bicycle race that takes place every year in France

Train à Grande Vitesse (trehn ah grawnd vee-TESS) Also known as TGV, fast trains that serve most of France

Versailles (vair-SIGH) A beautiful palace near Paris, where King Louis XIV lived

Vive la France (veeve lah frawnse) An expression that means "Long live France"

Index

 32